So Shy!

Illustrated by
Artkina Celestin

So Shy!
Text Copyright © 2022 by Elise Celestin
Illustrations Copyright © 2022 by Artkina Celestin
Published by Mo'ArtCee, LLC.
Printed in the United States

ISBN: 978-0-578-28380-7

Special thanks to Beryl Brackett of BAB Reviews for your help with editing!

Text set in Blueberry and Trochi. Illustrations created in Adobe Fresco and Procreate.
Book and Cover Design by Artkina Celestin set in Canva.

All rights reserved. No part of this publication may be reproduced in any form or by any means (including into electronic or mechanical storage or retrieval systems) without prior written authorization, except in the case of brief excerpts embodied in critical reviews and articles. Please submit all request for authorization to artkinacelestin@moartcee.com.

This book is dedicated to
all shy people, and to all my wonderful
friends and family who have helped me along
the way!
-Elise

There's a lump in my throat,

nothing comes up.

The words in my mouth,

I can't get them out.

When family is near, I'm loud and clear.

With others, I'm quiet and shy and I don't know why.

My legs get so stiff like they're stuck in the mud.

I want them to move but they just won't budge.

27)439

In class, when my teacher may ask for me to speak.

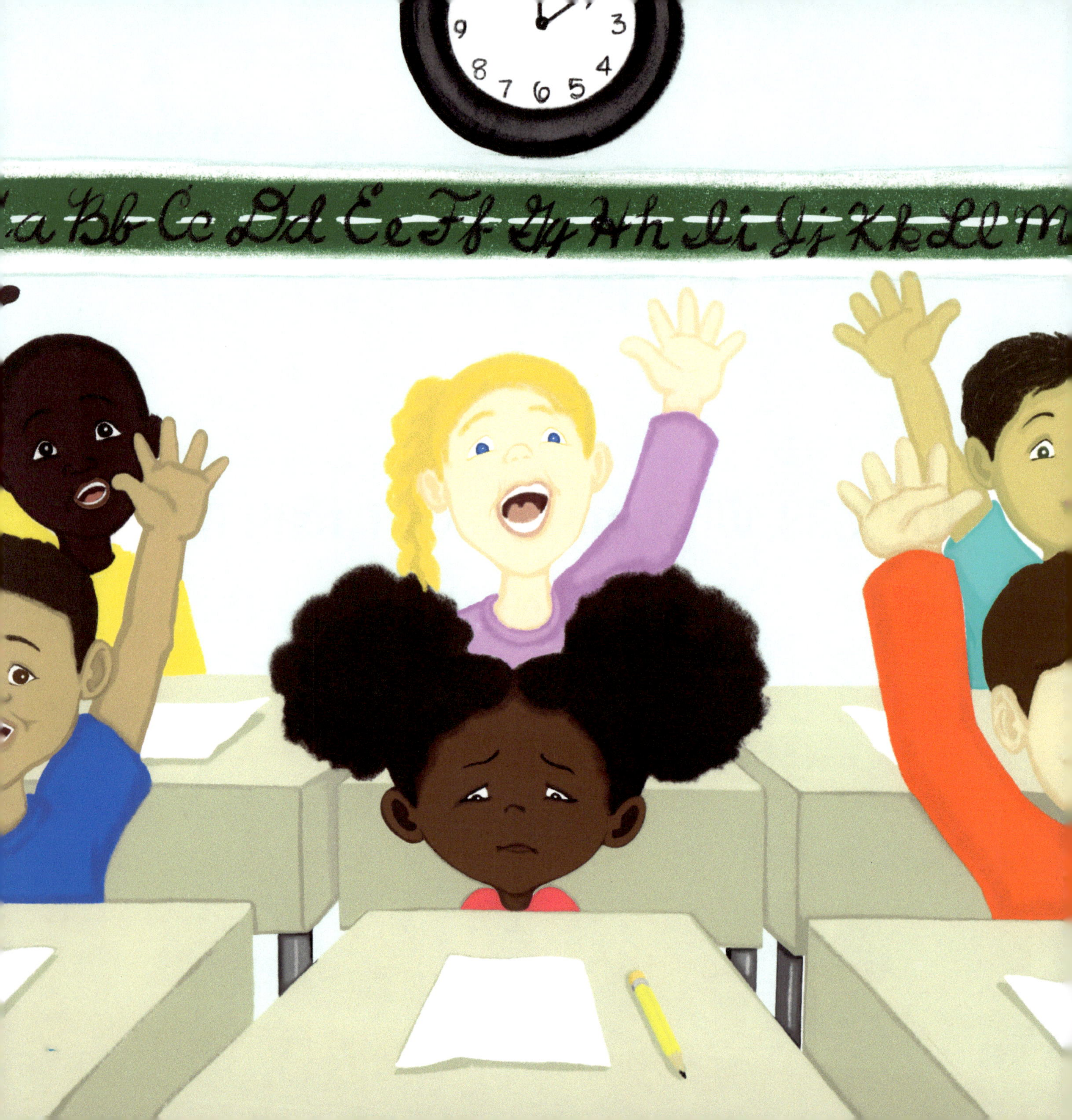
Bb Cc Dd Ee Ff Gg Hh Ii Jj Kk Ll

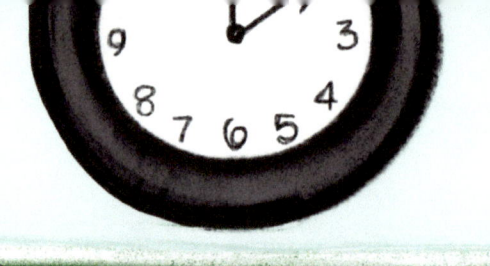

I shrink in my seat and can't make a peep.

At the lunch table, I don't think I'm able to join in all the fun.

Since talking to someone makes me want to run!

Kids are running here and there, laughing, playing everywhere, away from me without a care while I just sit and stare.

When I'm in band, I don't want to have to raise my hand.

Hoping I play perfectly so that no one stares at me.

Activities are fun

until...

you have to pair up with someone.

Not sure what to say or feel can leave me standing very still.

At the end of the day when the bus

oh how I hope that I can sit alone!

 This is what

it can  feel like

 to be so shy

when others don't always understand why and think that you don't want to try.

Elise Celestin is a fun loving, energetic, super imaginative ten-year-old girl who is on a mission to help people understand how difficult being shy can be. Elise wants people to know that it is ok to be shy! Within this last year she has been able to slowly come out of her shell. She loves making new friends, learning new things, and playing with her toys. "So Shy!" is Elise's first published book. She is super excited to share more of her stories and even wants to illustrate her own graphic novel.

CPSIA information can be obtained
at www.ICGtesting.com
Printed in the USA
BVHW021909190522
637508BV00002B/5